WORLD'S
CUTEST
ANIMALS

CONTENTS

(ANIMALS WITH A ★ NEXT TO THEIR NAME ARE EITHER ENDANGERED OR NEARLY ENDANGERED.)

ADORABILIS

These deep-sea octopi are so cute, a scientist called the species Adorabilis when she discovered it. See the two "ears" at the top of its head? Those are actually fins, and they have small webbed limbs for swimming, too.

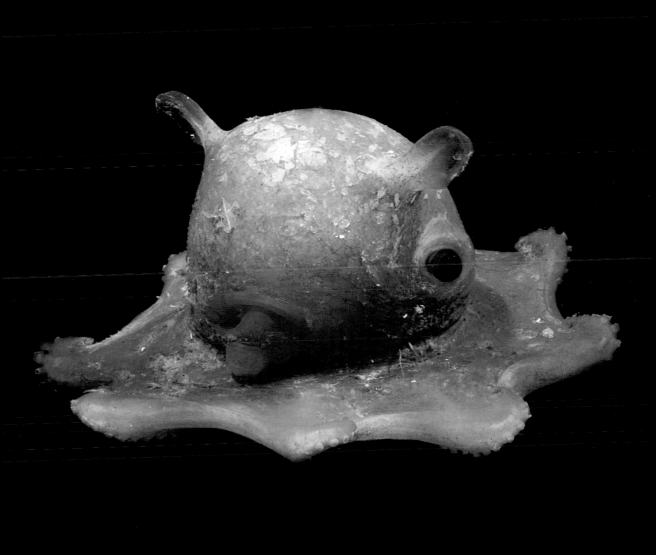

AMERICAN PIKA

Local to North America

Can you recognize this adorable creature? Many believe that Pikachu from the TV show *Pokémon* was based on the American pika. It turns out pikas make good friends in real life, too! Pikas will call out a warning when predators are near.

AXOLOTL ★

Local to North America

These salamanders never have to lose their baby faces! Axolotls have a special adaptation where they can choose when to grow up. Axolotls live underwater their entire lives, but if their home suddenly dries up, they just change into a form that survives on dry land.

BEE HUMMINGBIRD

Local to North America

Meet the smallest species of bird in the world. These hummingbirds are barely bigger than bees and they're often mistaken for bugs in the wild. Everything about this bird is mini! Even its eggs are about the size of green peas.

BLACK-FOOTED FERRET★
Local to North America

These cuties love to play! Baby black-footed ferrets have a dance for when they goof off. They arch their backs, open their mouths, and hop around backward from each other. Can you do the ferret dance?

BURROWING OWL

Local to North America

Burrowing owls get their name from the holes they tunnel down to live in. It seems like they're bobbing their heads as if saying hello. That's why cowboys used to call these friendly birds "Howdy Birds."

CALIFORNIA SEA LION

Local to North America

Even the sea lions in California love swimming and surfing. California sea lions take to the water so much, they can actually slow their heart rates in order to stay under for longer. They can hold their breath for 10 minutes or longer!

COYOTE

Local to North America

Coyotes are a lot like mini wolves. They hunt in packs, howl, yelp, and squeak to communicate with each other. Did you know coyotes can also mate with dogs? When a coyote and a dog pair, their babies are called "coydogs."

KIT FOX

Local to North America

They might be small, but they're fast! Kit foxes can run as fast as 25 miles per hour. They have extra fur on the bottom of their feet, which helps them run better over sand.

NORTHERN PYGMY OWL

Good things come to those who wait. Northern pygmy owls hunt by staying totally still and quiet. Then they swoop down and surprise their prey out of nowhere!

PRAIRIE DOG

Local to North America

Hey, these aren't dogs! They do sound like them though. Prairie dogs are actually rodents that communicate through a series of bark-like calls. They even use different calls for different predators, so they can let each other know exactly who's sneaking up on them.

SANDPIPER

Local to North America

These teeny shorebirds love chasing waves! Sandpipers pick through sand for tasty snacks like fish, snails, and larvae. Then when the waves come in, they have to run! It looks like they're just dashing back and forth, but they're only trying to eat in peace.

SNOWSHOE HARE

Local to North America

If a predator is near, these hares always bolt. Their feet are extra long and wide to help them dash better across the snow, and work like real-life snowshoes.

THINHORN SHEEP
Local to North America

Thinhorn sheep are really social and the lambs love to play! Young ones are always scrambling up and sliding down the mountain slopes where they live. But don't worry, the mother ewes are never far away.

TUFTED-TITMOUSE

Local to North America

Tufted titmice are like tiny gymnasts! These outgoing birds love hanging upside down from branches. They're known to visit bird feeders, so keep an eye out for these puffballs the next time you spot a feeder!

ALPACA
Local to South America

Alpacas have the cutest underbite! They don't have any front teeth in the top row. This is what gives them that million-dollar smile. They also have very soft, warm fur. Farmers have to shear the fleece just so they don't overheat in the summer!

BEARDED EMPEROR TAMARIN

Local to South America

Bearded emperor tamarins have more of an adorable-looking mustache than a beard. They live in the rainforest, and are very social animals that groom each other often. This strengthens bonds between the members of the group.

BIG-EARED OPOSSUM

Local to South America

Opossums often use the trick "playing dead." They ward off predators by flopping over and sticking out their tongues like they're dead. Nobody wants a meal that isn't fresh! Then when the coast is clear, opossums just pop right back up and go about their day.

BRAZILIAN PORCUPINE

Local to South America

They're cute, even if they're not exactly cuddly! Porcupines know how to fend for themselves. If they're scared, they rattle their spines and clack their teeth. Just a reminder to a predator that porcupines bite, too!

CAPYBARA

Local to South America

Capybaras are semiaquatic mammals that dive into water to escape predators. They can stay underwater for as long as five minutes. Like hippos, their eyes, ears, and nostrils are all near the top of their heads. So they need only pop up the slightest bit to catch a breath!

CHINCHILLA

Local to South America

Chinchillas love to explore! These adventurous animals use their long whiskers to help feel out their environments. When startled, these cuties spread their whiskers wide in shock.

GUANACO

Local to South America

If you think these guys kinda look like llamas, it's because they're related! Both are camelids, a group of animals that also includes alpacas. Newborn guanacos walk from the moment they're born. It's so they can always stick with the group.

LLAMA

Local to South America

Llamas are gentle animals. But they definitely get mad when humans give them too much stuff to carry. They lay down, hiss, and spit when they're upset. So don't ever take advantage of your llama pals!

MARMOSET

Local to South America

Marmosets are very social and family-oriented creatures. Couples mate for life and their older offspring help raise the younger ones. Marmosets also typically give birth to twins. So nobody's without a partner in crime, even from the beginning!

OCELOT

Local to South America

Ocelots are bigger than house cats, but not as big as leopards or tigers. These kitties also never roar like lions do. Instead, they make chuckling or muttering sounds when they're happy.

PATAGONIAN MARA

Local to South America

Patagonian maras are technically rodents, though they look more like small deer! These maras mate for life. Once they pair up, they do almost everything together and raise their young alongside other couples in large dens.

PUDU★
Local to South America

Say hello to the world's smallest deer! Pudus have short tails and legs to slip through underbrush more easily. They're so small they have to stand upright on their hind legs so they can nibble on hard-to-reach vegetation.

SOUTHERN TAMANDUA

Local to South America

Tamanduas may look adorable, but they also know how to defend themselves! If a predator attacks, tamanduas can hang upside down and use their powerful arms and claws to fight.

SOUTHERN VISCACHA

Local to South America

These cuties look a lot like rabbits, but they're actually rodents! At night, they hide from predators underground. In the daytime, their favorite activity is sunning themselves on a cozy rock perch.

SPECTACLED BEAR*

Local to South America

The whitish markings around these bears' eyes look almost like glasses. That's how these spectacled bears got their name. They may also be the most patient animals in the world. They actually wait for fruit to ripen before eating it!

EURASIAN LYNX

Local to Europe

These big cats have longer back legs than front legs, so they can pounce quickly to catch their prey. Lynxes hunt during the night, and at dawn and dusk. When it's light out, though, these hunters like a good nap under the bushes.

EUROPEAN HEDGEHOG

Local to Europe

Everyone knows these shy little cuties ball up into spiny spheres when they're scared. But you probably don't know how hedgehogs got their name. They make soft, snuffling sounds when they forage, just like pigs!

GOLDCREST

Local to Europe

These birds look just like little balls of fluff with tails and beaks attached because they have such short necks. But fearless goldcrests also build their nests at the tops of the tallest trees. They're as brave as they are cute.

HIGHLAND COW

Local to Europe

How do these cows keep their hair out of their faces? (They don't!) Highland cows have double-layered coats for extra warmth, and still manage to look good. These fashionistas definitely win the award for world's most luscious locks.

LONG-TAILED TIT

Local to Europe

These birds have tails that are longer than their tiny bodies. When they're cold, they huddle together in a tight ball—like one giant cuddle puddle!

PINE MARTEN

Local to Europe

Pine martens have retractable claws that they use for climbing and running across trees! They have very sensitive ears that help them hunt at night.

SAIGA ANTELOPE★

Local to Europe

These animals have huge noses! Their trunk-like sniffers filter out dust while they graze in the hot summer months. And in the winter, these noses help warm the air they breathe.

AARDWOLF

Local to Africa

The aardwolf's name means "earth wolf" in Afrikaans, a language spoken in Southern Africa. They mostly eat termites. With sticky tongues and peg-like teeth, they have the perfect tools to munch on insects!

AFRICAN HARE

Local to Africa

African hares have big ears to help hear predators from faraway distances. Sometimes their ears are longer than their body! These quick rabbits can run as fast as 43 miles per hour.

AFRICAN HELMETED TURTLE

Local to Africa

African helmeted turtles bury their whole bodies in mud to protect themselves. When found above ground, they look like they're smiling—like they're happy to see you!

AFRICAN SAVANNA ELEPHANT*

Local to Africa

Elephants use advanced vocalizations to call out to each other. They can recognize who's who from over a mile away! Multiple families will join together in groups of more than 100 elephants, led by one female.

BAT-EARED FOX

Local to Africa

These foxes use their huge, bat-like ears to listen out for predators . . . and bugs. Their diet consists mostly of termites.

BLACK-FOOTED CAT*

Local to Africa

This is one of the world's smallest wild cat species. What they lack in size they make up for in spirit! Black-footed cats are known to scare off much larger predators. Go little one, go!

BUSHB**UCK**

Local to Africa

These shy grazers earned their name from where they like to forage for food or hide from predators: the bush! If they're caught by surprise in the open, they'll freeze or walk calmly to the bushes for cover.

DIBATAG★
Local to Africa

These antelopes will hide in vegetation and stay very still when they're spooked. They have long necks and stick their heads up to check if the coast is clear.

ETHIOPIAN WOLF*

Local to Africa

These wolves travel in packs and form very strong bonds with one another. They patrol their territory at dawn and dusk, and spend their nights cuddling together under the stars.

FENNEC FOX
Local to Africa

Fennec foxes are specially adapted for the desert. Their big, batty ears can grow up to half their size, and release heat to keep their bodies cool. They also have extra-hairy feet to protect them from the hot sand.

MASAI GIRAFFE

Local to Africa

his is the largest species of giraffe. What also sets these giraffes apart from other types is the leafy pattern of their spots. Masai giraffes choose snacking over napping, and can eat continuously for 16—20 hours a day!

MEERKAT

Local to Africa

Meerkats are some of the most cooperative animals. They work in groups as large as 50 and take turns foraging for food. They live underground in tunnel systems called burrows, where they can stay safe from predators and keep cool during hot days.

OKAPI★

Local to Africa

Don't judge okapis by their stripes! They may look like zebras, but they're related to giraffes. They don't have long necks like giraffes or live in the savanna. They actually live in the rain forest—where there are lots of leaves to eat from low-hanging branches.

PYGMY HIPPO-POTAMUS★

Local to Africa

The look of their teeth and tusks would send anyone running. But pygmy hippopotamuses are 10 times lighter than their larger relatives. They're also shyer and much less aggressive.

SPRINGBOK

Local to Africa

When springboks get excited, they "pronk." This is a type of jumping that displays the fluff of soft, white hair along their backs. It almost looks like they're doing ballet!

BINTURONG★

Local to Asia

Binturong are also called "bearcats," because they look a little bit like cats and also a little bit like bears. But they're not actually related to either! Binturong have a unique scent: they smell like buttered popcorn. Though pleasing to humans, this odor keeps other animals away.

BORNEO PYGMY ELEPHANT*

Local to Asia

Borneo pygmy elephants are the smallest species of elephant. Even the adults look like babies! Their tails are so long, they actually drag along the ground as they walk.

IRRAWADDY DOLPHIN★
Local to Asia

}rrawaddy dolphins have round heads and no beaks, and they're always smiling! But don't be deceived by their cute faces. These dolphins like to spit water, usually to herd fish and make them easier to catch.

JAPANESE DWARF FLYING SQUIRREL

Local to Asia

These squirrels can glide over distances as far as 500 feet, but they're small enough to fit in your hand. They sleep curled up in trees during the day, and their huge eyes help them see at night.

KIANG

Local to Asia

These adorable grazers look like small horses with their short ears, long tails, and manes. But they're actually a species of wild donkey. Kiangs are super tight-knit. They'll travel long distances in search of food and stay together the whole way.

LEOPARD CAT

Local to Asia

Leopard cats are only as big as house cats! In fact, they are thought to be the first cats kept as pets by humans. They love to swim and have been known to paddle toward islands that they claim for themselves.

MALAYAN SUN BEAR*

Local to Asia

uess how these bears got their name? It's because the marks on their chests look like the sun! Malayan sun bears like to cradle cubs in their arms, just like humans do.

MALAYAN TAPIR★

Local to Asia

These animals have long, trunk-like noses like elephants, which they use to pull branches, leaves, and fruit from trees. They can also use their noses as snorkels to breathe underwater.

MANDARIN DUCK

Local to Asia

Male mandarin ducks (known as drakes) shimmy, preen, and fluff their feathers during courting rituals! When these ducks pair up, they often stay together for many seasons.

MUNTJAC DEER
Local to Asia

Muntjac deer let out low alarm barks to scare off predators when they sense danger. That's why they're nicknamed the "barking deer." They have teeth like sharp little tusks, so they're as fierce as they are cute!

PHILIPPINE FLYING LEMUR

Local to Asia

These misnamed animals aren't really lemurs and they don't really fly. They actually glide from tree to tree in the forest. They're so good at it, mothers can carry their young on their backs as they soar through the air.

PRZEWALSKI'S HORSE★

Local to Asia

These mini horses can be found grazing in national parks and reserves in Central Asia. They're the last surviving species of wild horse in the world. They're shorter and squatter than domesticated horses.

RED PANDA★

Local to Asia

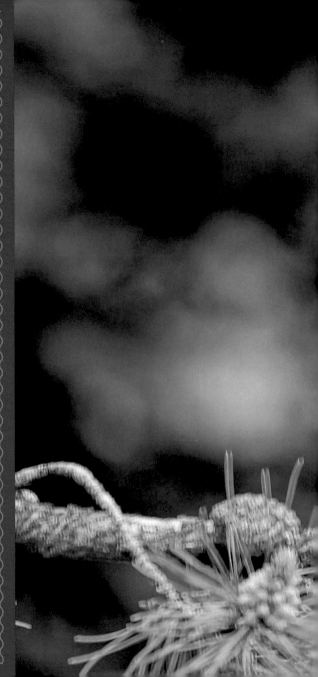

Red pandas eat lots of bamboo. They're also expert climbers and spend most of their time in the trees—even when they eat and sleep! They wrap themselves in their big, fluffy tails to keep warm at night.

SIBERIAN CHIPMUNK

Local to Asia

Siberian chipmunks are good little diggers. They make huge underground burrows for themselves, and fill them up with food to last them while they hibernate all winter long. They only wake up to snack before snuggling back down to sleep.

SLOW LORIS★

Local to Asia

Slow lorises may look sweet, but they're actually one of the few types of mammals with a venomous bite. Slow lorises will even lick their young to cover them in the toxin, so predators think twice before trying to eat them.

'URAL OWL

Local to Asia

Did you know birds have singing contests? These owls love to see who sings best, especially when they're looking for a partner. Couples even sing duets when they find their perfect match.

WALLACE'S FLYING FROG
Local to Asia

These adventurous amphibians have a secret trick. They can fly! Well, sort of. When they jump and spread all four of their webbed feet at once, they can travel up to 50 feet in the air. Their feet act as wings!

DINGO★

Local to Australia

Dingoes look like dogs but act more like wolves. They live and hunt in packs, and howl instead of bark. They don't sleep through the night, but sleep every few hours—napping and hunting around the clock!

KANGAROO

Local to Australia

Kangaroos belong to an animal family called *Macropodidae*. This translates loosely as "big foot." These feet allow Kangaroos to leap up to 30 feet in one bound and travel as fast as 30 miles per hour.

KIWI★

Local to New Zealand

Kiwis have tiny wings that blend right into their brown, fuzzy feathers and round bodies. Kiwifruit, which are also brown, fuzzy, and round, got their name from these cuties.

KOALA★

Local to Australia

I't's a pretty sweet life for baby koalas. Koala moms nurse their young in pouches for the first few months after birth. Even after they can leave the pouch, koala babies climb onto their mother's backs and ride along there. They do this until they're almost a year old!

LITTLE BLUE PENGUIN

Local to Australia

These are the world's smallest penguins! Named for their size and bluish coloring, they're also called fairy penguins. Even fully grown, these birds only stand about 12 inches tall and weigh around three pounds.

MOUNTAIN PYGMY POSSUM★

Local to Australia

These mouselike possums have a clever tactic for staying warm. They burrow under snow! Mountain pygmy possums have such thick fur that the snow becomes just another layer of insulation. It's almost like a fluffy blanket!

NEW ZEALAND FUR SEAL

Local to New Zealand

*O*ut of all the fur seals, New Zealand fur seals can dive the deepest and for the longest time! These accomplished swimmers can stay underwater for as long as **14 minutes!**

QUOKKA★

Local to Australia

Quokkas are about the size of cats and hop like kangaroos. They burrow underground for quick naps. Don't expect to win a game of hide-and-seek with a quokka . . . you might be seeking for a while!

SPOTTED-TAIL QUOLL★

Local to Australia

Spotted-tail quolls hunt at night and are most active after sunset. Many nocturnal creatures like to den underground during the day, but spotted-tail quolls prefer snoozing under the sun and absorbing its heat.

TREE KANGAROO★
Local to Australia

These cuties are exactly what they sound like: mini kangaroos that live in trees! Tree kangaroos feed mostly on leaves, bark, moss, and flowers, and can fall as far as 60 feet to the ground without injury.

TUATARA ★
Local to New Zealand

Did you know tuatara translates to "spiny back" in Maori, the language of New Zealand's native people! Tuataras are considered "living fossils" because they are the only surviving members of a group of reptiles that lived over 200 million years ago!

WOMBAT★

Wombats are real homebodies. They'll build a whole underground network of tunnels and chambers just for themselves! But some species are more sociable, and share their underground networks to form colonies.

ARTIC FOX
Local to the Arctic Circle

Arctic foxes use their bushy tails for balance and warmth. These cuddly foxes wrap their tails around themselves when cold and can survive temperatures down to -58°F!

ARCTIC HARE

Local to the Arctic Circle

Arctic hares live in the frozen tundra, where temperatures reach as low as -72°F. They often bury themselves underneath snow, huddling with other bunnies in order to stay warm!

ARCTIC LEMMING

Local to the Arctic Circle

Lemmings don't hibernate. During the winter, they dig burrows for shelter and use their thick fur to keep warm. They are excellent at scrounging around in the snow for bulbs and shoots to eat.

EMPEROR PENGUIN
Local to Antarctica

These birds don't fly—but they swim! When they're out of the water they huddle to keep warm in freezing temperatures. They even rotate positions so the ones in the center don't get too hot . . . in the middle of an Antarctica winter!

POLAR BEAR★

Local to the Arctic Circle

Polar bears like to play, too! Sibling cubs chase and tackle each other. When polar bears want to play with one another, they might wag their heads from side to side.

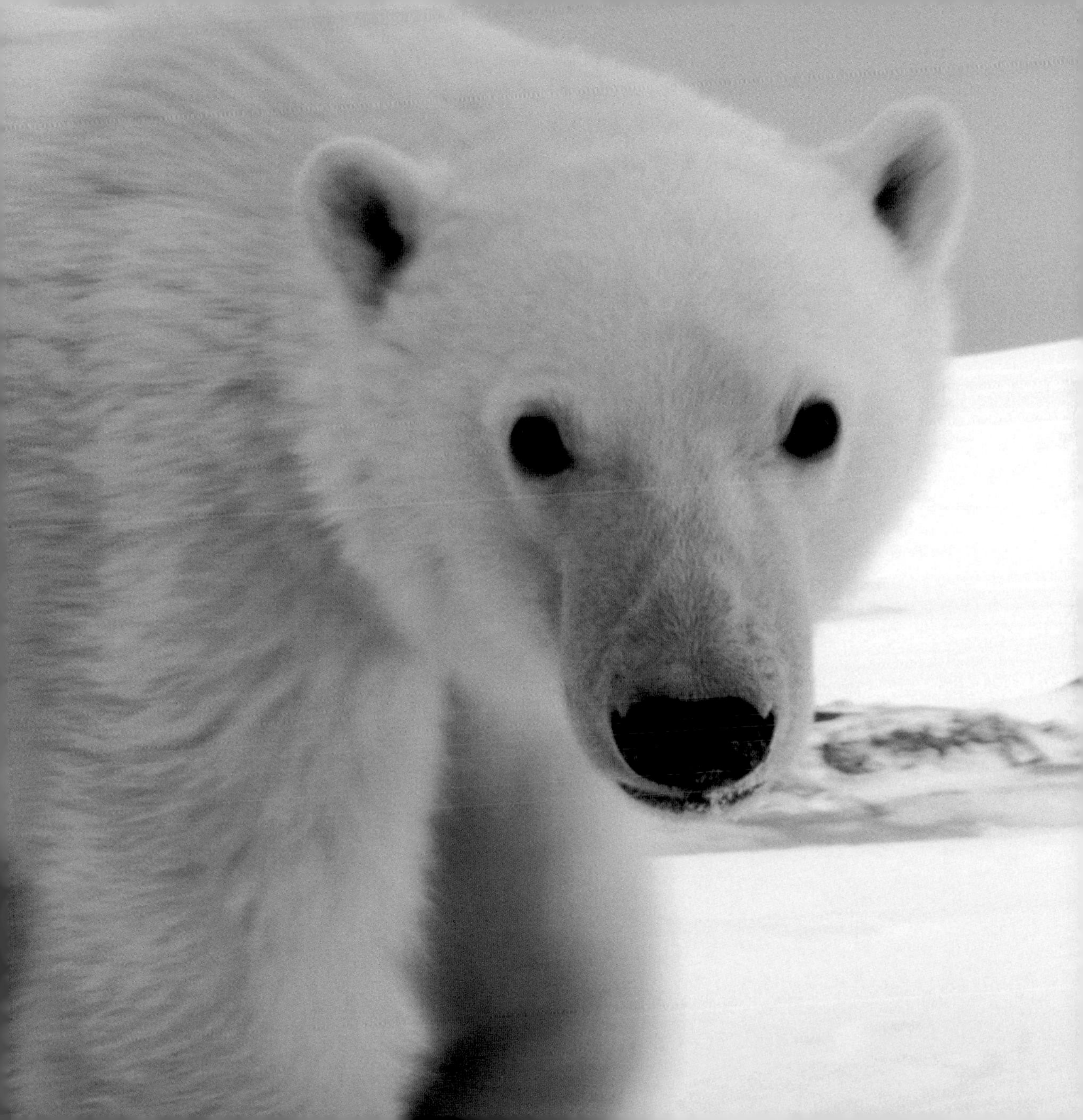

PUFFIN ★

Local to the Arctic Circle

Don't let the expression fool you! Puffins are very efficient hunters. They have spines on their upper beak and tongue, which are perfect for catching fish. And they can carry an average of 10 fish in their bill at once!

BOTTLENOSE DOLPHIN

Found in worldwide waters

These dolphins each come with a theme song! Bottlenose dolphins use unique whistles to both identify themselves and recognize one another. This helps them travel, hunt, and play together all their lives.

DORMOUSE

Local to Africa, Asia, and Europe

This is the world's sleepiest mouse! Dormice can hibernate for as long as seven months out of the year. That's probably where the inspiration for the sleeping dormouse in *Alice in Wonderland* came from.

DUGONG*

Local to Africa, Asia, and Australia

Dugongs eat only sea grasses at the bottom of shallow waters. But every once in a while they have to come up for air. Sometimes dugongs "stand" on their tails, peeking just the tip of their heads above water to breathe.

HAWKSBILL TURTLE★
Local to Atlantic and Pacific Oceans

Hawksbill turtles have shells shaped like hearts, which nature decorated with a beautiful, distinctive pattern. Like most sea turtles, hawksbills always return to the same place they were born to lay their eggs.

IBEX

Local to Africa, Asia, and Europe

These mountain goats are right at home on the rockiest cliffs. They escape predators simply by climbing where they can't be followed! Ibex have hooves that work like suction cups, which make them such great climbers.

KENTISH PLOVER

Local to Africa, Asia, Europe, North America, and South America

These birds don't build nests, they dig them! That's why their homes are called "scrapes." They scrape a small hole in sand or dirt close to the water, which is also where they like to feed.

MANATEE★

Found in worldwide waters

These gentle giants are aquatic-based herbivores. That means they only eat plants! As slow as they are sweet, manatees typically glide at a speed of only five miles per hour.

MOOSE

Local to the Arctic Circle, Asia, Europe, and North America

Moose have thick skin adapted for cold weather. But this means they get hot! In warm weather, they are often found swimming in lakes or ponds to stay cool.

PORCUPINE PUFFER FISH

Found in worldwide waters

When these fish puff up, their spines stick out in every direction! They've got cute smiles, but they also want predators to know they'd make for a terrible meal. No one wants a side of spines with their food!

REINDEER★

Local to Europe and North America

Have you heard of reindeer races? In Scandinavia, people celebrate Sami culture by racing reindeer against each other! These elegant animals have cloven hooves that help them walk and run faster over snow. In the wild, this helps them escape predators. In racing, it helps them win!

SEA OTTER★

Local to Asia and North America

Napping is hard in the ocean! That doesn't stop these sleepy sea otters from trying. A mother and her pup will hold hands to keep from drifting away from each other. Sea otters also wrap themselves in kelp when they want to anchor themselves in place.

SLOTH★

Local to North and South America

Sloths sleep as if their lives depend on it! Snoozing up to 20 hours a day, they hardly move even while awake. Sloths' coats are covered with rich green algae, which they may eat to add nutrients to their diet of leaves. It's like they carry around their lunch on their fur!

STOAT

Local to Asia, Europe, and North America

Stoats don't always chase their prey. Sometimes they dance! Their random, bouncing movements can trick animals into standing still. They probably just can't believe how bad stoats are at dancing.

AUTHOR'S NOTE

Every animal in this book with a ★ next to its name is either endangered or vulnerable to becoming endangered. This means their numbers are decreasing, mostly due to pollution, habitat loss, overhunting and overfishing, or climate change. All of these environmental problems have been caused by humans.

But there are ways you can help. Visit the websites below to learn more about how you can get involved.

WORLD WILDLIFE FUND
worldwildlife.org

NATURAL RESOURCES DEFENSE COUNCIL
nrdc.org

WILDLIFE CONSERVATION SOCIETY
wcs.org

RAINFOREST ACTION NETWORK
ran.org

NATURE CONSERVANCY
nature.org

PHOTO CREDITS

Cover: Floridapfe from S.Korea Kim in cherl/Getty Images (fennec fox); Karl Burry/Shutterstock (giraffe); James Hager/Getty Images (America pika); Popmarleo/Getty Images (scallop pattern); **3:** Richard Peterson/Shutterstock / **4-5 (and throughout):** Popmarleo/Getty Images (pattern) / **7:** Dante Fenolio/Science Photo Library / **8 (and throughout):** milezaway/Shutterstock (pattern) / **9:** James Hager/Getty Images / **11:** GlobalP/Getty Images / **13:** Melinda Fawver/Shutterstock / **14:** miakievy/Getty Images (pattern) / **15:** Jeff Vanuga/Getty Images / **17:** mlorenzphotography/Getty Images / **19:** Eric Isselee/Shutterstock / **21:** Bryan Bailey/Shutterstock / **23:** Max Allen/Shutterstock / **25:** Feng Yu/Shutterstock / **27:** Gary Parnell/EyeEm/Getty Images / **29:** sysasya photography/Shutterstock / **31:** Martin Smart/Alamy Stock Photo / **33:** Heiti Paves/Alamy Stock Photo / **35:** Ed Reschke/Getty Images / **37:** Pat Gaines/Getty Images / **39:** AlexTurton/Getty Images / **41:** Leonardo Mercon/Shutterstock / **43:** www.bartvandorp.com/Getty Images / **45:** Chris Brunskill Ltd/Getty Images / **47:** Artverau/Shutterstock / **49:** Ionov Vitaly/Shutterstock / **51:** imageBROKER/Alamy Stock Photo / **53:** Mark Finney/Getty Images / **55:** Leonardo Mercon/Shutterstock / **57:** Stuart Fuidge/Shutterstock / **59:** imageBROKER/Alamy Stock Photo / **61:** Eric Isselee/Shutterstock / **63:** Jonathan Chancasana/500px / **65:** Juniors Bildarchiv GmbH/Alamy Stock Photo / **67:** Nagel Photography/Shutterstock / **69:** Richard Peterson/Shutterstock / **71:** Gary Chalker/Getty Images / **73:** Markus Gr_wers/EyeEm/Getty Images / **75:** Gary Chalker/Getty Images / **77:** Ghost Bear/Shutterstock / **79:** Nature Picture Library/Alamy Stock Photo / **81:** pjmalsbury/Getty Images / **83:** Maggy Meyer/Shutterstock / **85:** Bildagentur Zoonar GmbH/Shutterstock / **87:** All Canada Photos/Alamy Stock Photo / **89:** Danita Delimont/Alamy Stock Photo / **91:** Tom Brakefield/Getty Images / **93:** SAPhotog/Shutterstock / **95:** LagunaticPhoto/Shutterstock / **97:** Avalon/Photoshot License/Alamy Stock Photo / **99:** Floridapfe from S.Korea Kim in cherl/Getty Images / **101:** Karl Burry/Shutterstock / **103:** irawansubingarphotography/Shutterstock / **105:** Eric Isselee/Shutterstock / **107:** bunyarit/Shutterstock / **109:** Luca Roggero/EyeEm/Getty Images / **111:** tomava/Shutterstock / **113:** feathercollector/Shutterstock / **115:** Gerard Soury/Getty Images / **117:** keiichihiki/Getty Images / **119:** blickwinkel/Alamy Stock Photo / **121:** Rosa Jay/Shutterstock / **123:** DPL/Alamy Stock Photo / **125:** David & Micha Sheldon/Getty Images / **127:** Edwin Godinho/EyeEm/ Getty Images / **129:** Christopher Cook/Alamy Stock Photo / **131:** Tlapy007/Shutterstock / **133:** Yuri Shebalius/Shutterstock / **135:** Simone Torkington/EyeEm/Getty Images / **137:** stock_shot/Shutterstock / **139:** Hoang Mai Thach/Shutterstock / **141:** Jacek Kadaj/Getty Images / **143:** irawansubingarphotography/Getty Images / **145:** Doug Gimesy/Getty Images / **147:** John White Photos/Getty Images / **149:** Eric Isselee/Shutterstock / **151:** Michael Siward/Getty Images / **153:** Shannon Hibberd/Alamy Stock Photo / **155:** Jason Edwards/Getty Images / **157:** tubblefield Photography/Shutterstock / **159:** Luca Diehl/Shutterstock / **161:** Eric Isselee/Shutterstock / **163:** Brad Leue/Alamy Stock Photo / **165:** Alizada Studios/Shutterstock / **167:** Tier Und Naturfotografie J und C Sohns/Getty Images / **169:** DmitryND/Getty Images / **171:** Design Pics Inc/Alamy Stock Photo / **173:** Frank Fichtmueller/Shutterstock / **175:** Frank Krahmer/Getty Images / **177:** Daniel J. Cox/Getty Images /

179: Livia Lazar/EyeEm/Getty Images / **181:** rohojamic/Getty Images / **183:** Fabrizio Moglia/Getty Images / **185:** Alex Churilov/Shutterstock / **187:** Sirachai Arunrugstichai/Getty Images / **189:** blickwinkel/Alamy Stock Photo / **191:** Premium Stock Photography GmbH/Alamy Stock Photo / **193:** 33karen33/Getty Images / **195:** Volodymyr Burdiak/Shutterstock / **197:** gorosan/Shutterstock / **199:** Jellis Vaes/Shutterstock / **201:** Tim Laman/Getty Images / **203:** www.bartvandorp.com/GettyImages / **205:** Miroslav Hlavko/Shutterstock

ACKNOWLEDGMENTS

Publishing Director: Piers Pickard / **Publisher:** Hanna Otero / **Editor:** Rhoda Belleza / **Author:** Anna Poon / **Art Director:** Ryan Thomann / **Print Production:** Lisa Ford

Published in April 2019 by Lonely Planet Global Limited
CRN: 554153
ISBN: 978-1-78868-125-4
www.lonelyplanetkids.com
© Lonely Planet 2019

Printed in China
10 9 8 7 6

STAY IN TOUCH - lonelyplanet.com/contact

Lonely Planet Office:
IRELAND Digital Depot, Roe Lane (off Thomas St),
Digital Hub, Dublin 8, D08 TCV4, Ireland

Paper in this book is certified against the Forest Stewardship Council™ standards. FSC™ promotes environmentally responsible, socially beneficial and economically viable management of the world's forests.